Library of Congress Cataloging-in-Publication Data

Thomson, Ruth.
All About 1, 2, 3.

(My first easy and fun books)
Summary: The reader is asked to help Sam find one armadillo, two jaguars, and other jungle animals, counting
from one up to ten, and to point out which animals are performing certain activities such as swimming, eating
berries, and sticking their tongues out.
1. Literary recreations. [1. Literary recreations. 2. Counting. 3. Jungle animals--Fiction] I. Ursell, Martin, ill. II. Title.
III. Title: One, two, three. IV. Series: Thomson, Ruth. My first easy and fun books.
PZ7.T38Aac 1987 [E] 87-42593
ISBN 1-55532-341-3
ISBN 1-55532-316-2 (lib. bdg.)

North American edition first published in 1987 by
Gareth Stevens, Inc.
7221 West Green Tree Road Milwaukee, WI 53223, USA

First published as *1 2 3* in the United Kingdom by Walker Books Ltd.

Typeset by Web Tech, Inc., Milwaukee. Printed in Italy.
Series Editor: MaryLee Knowlton.

1 2 3 4 5 6 7 8 9 92 91 90 89 88 87

MY FIRST EASY AND FUN BOOKS

ALL ABOUT

1 2 3

By Ruth Thomson
Illustrated by Martin Ursell

Gareth Stevens Publishing
Milwaukee

Today Sam is going into
the jungle to look at animals.

Can you see **one**
armadillo looking at Sam?

Jaguars climb trees in the jungle.
Help Sam find **two** jaguars.

How many jaguars have spots?
How many are asleep?

Alligators always live near water.
Help Sam find **three** alligators.

How many of them are swimming?
How many are sunbathing?

Toucans have huge beaks.
Help Sam find **four** toucans.

How many toucans are eating?
Which one has the most berries?

Tree frogs are brightly colored.
Help Sam find **five** tree frogs.

How many are jumping?
How many have green legs?

Snakes have forked tongues.
Help Sam find **six** snakes.

How many snakes have their tongues
out? How many are on the ground?

7

Parrots live high in the trees.
Help Sam find **seven** parrots.

How many parrots are flying?
How many have red tail feathers?

Monkeys swing from branch to branch.
Help Sam find **eight** monkeys.

How many monkeys have bananas?
How many are hanging by their tails?

Butterflies have wings made of tiny
scales. Help Sam find **nine** butterflies.

How many are resting on leaves? How many have eyespots on their wings?

The spiders come out at sundown.
Help Sam find **ten** spiders.

How many spiders are hairy?
How many are making webs?

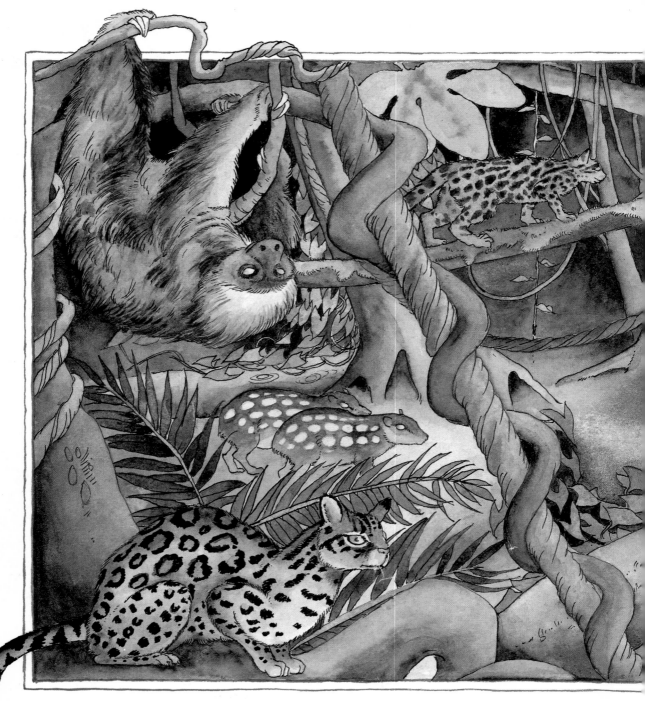

Sam is fast asleep now in his tent. But all the night animals are wide awake.

How many animals can you see?

Here are all the animals Sam has seen.

1	**one** armadillo	
2	**two** jaguars	
3	**three** alligators	
4	**four** toucans	
5	**five** tree frogs	

6	six snakes	
7	seven parrots	
8	eight monkeys	
9	nine butterflies	
10	ten spiders	

Things To Do

1. Watch a tree in your yard or a park for 5 - 10 minutes. Count the birds that fly into it.

2. In the kitchen:

   Read the numbers on gauges, dials, and temperature indicators of these appliances in your kitchen:

   stove   refrigerator
   microwave   measuring cups
              measuring spoons

3. Count the number of red cars that pass your house in five minutes. Then count black or blue or gray. What color cars do you see the most?

4. Line up empty milk cartons or soda cans. Roll a ball to knock them down. Count how many you knock down.

5. When you're riding in a car find license plates that begin with each number in order from 1 through 9. You can go higher if your trip is long. Call out the number when you see it.

6. When you start on a car trip, decide what color things to count. Everybody can look for things and call out what they see.

7. Eat some watermelon. Count the seeds.

8. Draw numbers on a friend's back with your fingers. Have her or him tell you what number you drew. Take turns.

More Books About 1 2 3

*Animal 1*2*3!* Lee (Gareth Stevens)

Anno's Counting Book. Anno (Harper & Row)

Cat Count. Lewin (Dodd, Mead)

Count and See. Hoban (Macmillan)

Goodnight Hattie, My Dearie, My Dove. Schertle (Lothrop, Lee & Shepard)

How Much Is a Million? Schwartz (Lothrop, Lee & Shepard)

Max's Toys. Wells (Dial)

Mouse Count! Law and Chandler (Gareth Stevens)

Twenty-one Balloons. Dubois (Dell)

Twenty-six Starlings Will Fly Through Your Mind. Wersba (Harper & Row)

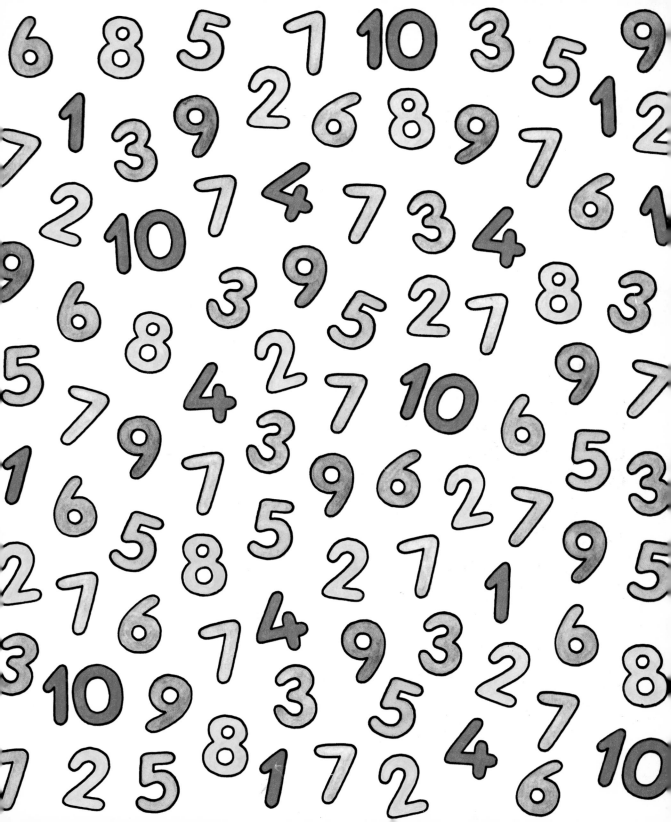